ENERGY, LIGHT AND ELECTRICITY

INTRODUCTION TO PHYSICS

Physics Book for 12 Year Old

Children's Physics Books

BABY PROFESSOR
EDUCATION KIDS

Speedy Publishing LLC

40 E. Main St. #1156

Newark, DE 19711

www.speedypublishing.com

Copyright 2017

In this book, we're going to talk about energy, light, and electricity. So, let's get right to it!

If you go outside on a sunny day, you'll see lots of different things. Suppose you look at a flowering plant. You're able to see the flower on the plant because energy from the sun in the form of light has traveled down to Earth. This sunlight is what makes it possible for your eyes to see the flower.

However, if you go outdoors at night, it will be much more difficult for you to see unless there's a bright, full moon outdoors. If you go inside a building after dark, you won't be able to see much of anything if you don't have artificial light.

The famous inventor Thomas Edison perfected the light bulb. He thought that once electricity was everywhere people would rarely sleep. It's definitely true that people do much more at nighttime than they did before there were electric lights.

light bulb

There are four common ways for us to create artificial light and three of them use electricity or battery power.

FIRE AND CANDLES

Before there were electric lights, people used fireplaces and candles indoors for lighting. Your home might have a fireplace and you might use candles for special occasions. Although it's pretty simple to strike a match to light a candle or to start a fire in your fireplace, the physics behind the creation of fire and the light it gives off isn't so simple.

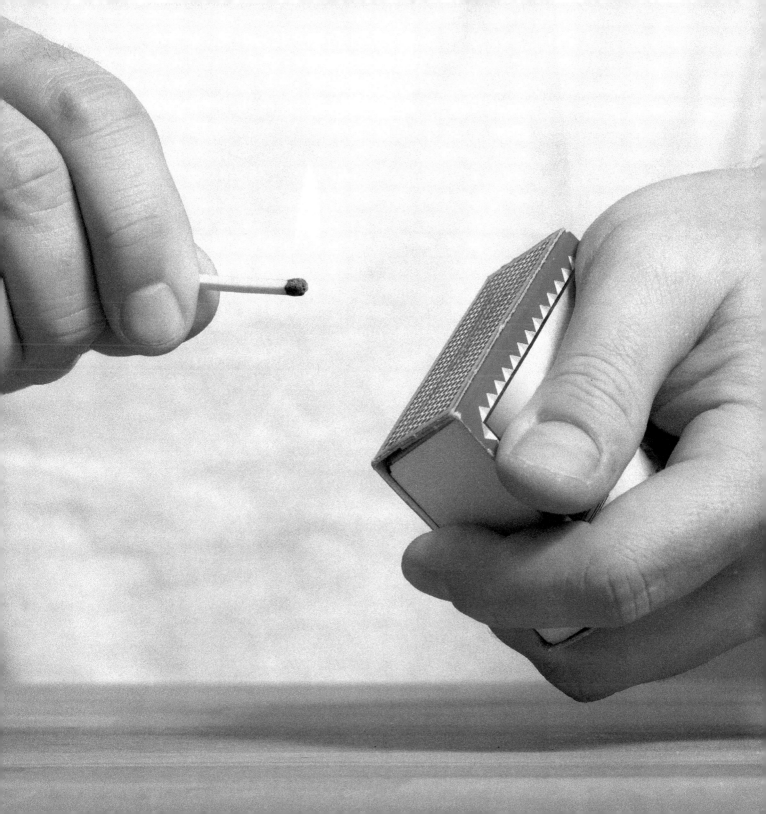

Things that burn, like pieces of wood, pieces of coal, or oil, all contain the element of carbon. That carbon is part of the composition of the molecules of the material that burns. Carbon can join with oxygen to form the end product of carbon dioxide. It takes energy to disengage carbon away from the bonds it has in the original material.

When carbon dioxide is created, it also creates excess energy. This is the basic physics behind how fire works. Beginning with some energy, you can transform carbon from organic materials into the compound of carbon and oxygen called carbon dioxide.

So, why does light show up when things are burning? The reason is that there are other materials being produced in addition to the carbon dioxide. These pieces of material that haven't burned are called soot. This soot rises along with the heated air above the area where the combustion has taken place. Since that soot has been heated, it produces light that we can see in the visible spectrum just like the filament in a light bulb does.

For hundreds of thousands of years, fire and candles were the only means of artificial light. However, there are issues with burning fires indoors. The environment gets hot, which might be fine during the winter, but not during the summer.

fireplace

Fire produces carbon dioxide and sucks the oxygen we need to breathe so it has to be carefully controlled. The other serious problem is that sometimes, if fire gets out of control, it can burn down your house.

LIGHT EMITTING DIODE (LED)

The light emitting diode, LED for short, was introduced in the 1960s and is used in many different devices today. Anytime that anything electronic lights up, there's a good chance that it contains an LED.

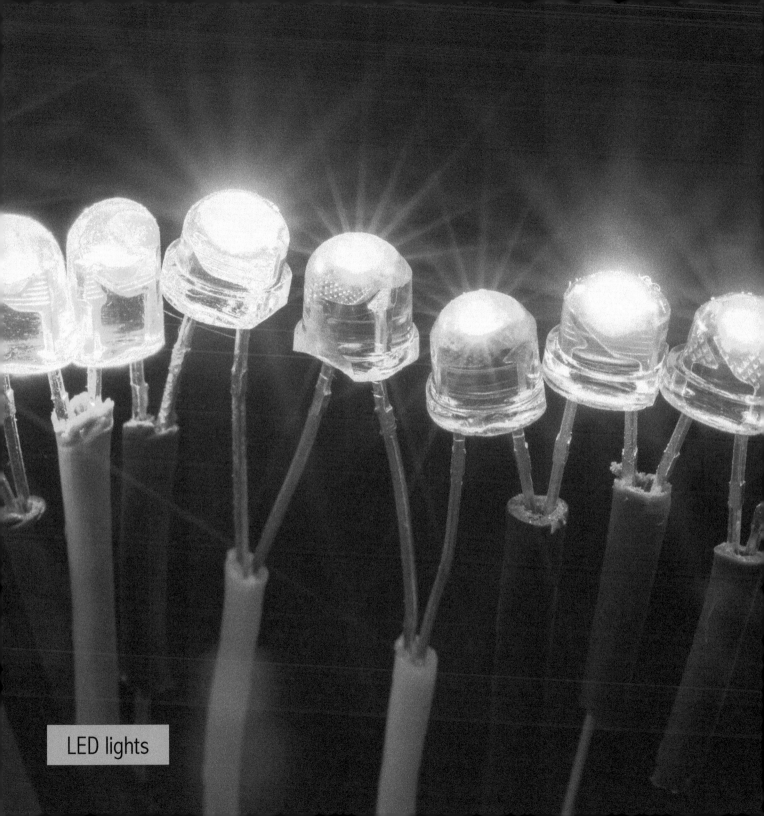

LED lights

TV remote control

The infrared television remote control, the light source for the camera in your smartphone, and a digital clock on your nightstand all contain LEDs.

The methods of producing light all have a major factor in common. At the atomic level, they all involve electrons that are changing their energy levels. When an electron changes from an energy level that's high to an energy level that's low, it creates light. The light's frequency is in direct proportion to the change in energy. We see these different light frequencies as light that is different colors within the spectrum of electromagnetic waves.

The LED doesn't use a chemical reaction. It doesn't use a mechanical method either. Instead, it's a type of device called a solid state device. It's a combination of two different types of materials that are semiconductors. Within these materials, the electrons move around at different levels of energy. As the electrons move across this energy gap, they create a specific color of light.

The first LED lights just created infrared light, which humans can't see. Eventually, red and green LEDs were created. Then, a blue LED was developed by combining different types of semiconductors. With the addition of blue, RGB (red, green, blue) lights could be made for video and computer displays. The development of blue LED opened the door to the creation of LED that looks white and can be used for lights.

LED lights have some great advantages. They are small and if you don't run too much electricity through them, they can last a very long time. They don't break if you shake them either. LED lights are also very energy efficient. The only downside is that they are more expensive for larger devices, but the prices are beginning to come down as the technology improves.

FLUORESCENT AND COMPACT FLUORESCENT

Fluorescent lights have been around since the 1950s. At the beginning, they were mostly used to light up industrial spaces in long, overhead fixtures, but today they are used in homes as well. Compact fluorescent lights are those spiral-shaped lights that you can use to replace a more traditional incandescent light bulb. They are designed to fit in lamps and other sockets where incandescent lights were always used before.

compact flourescent light

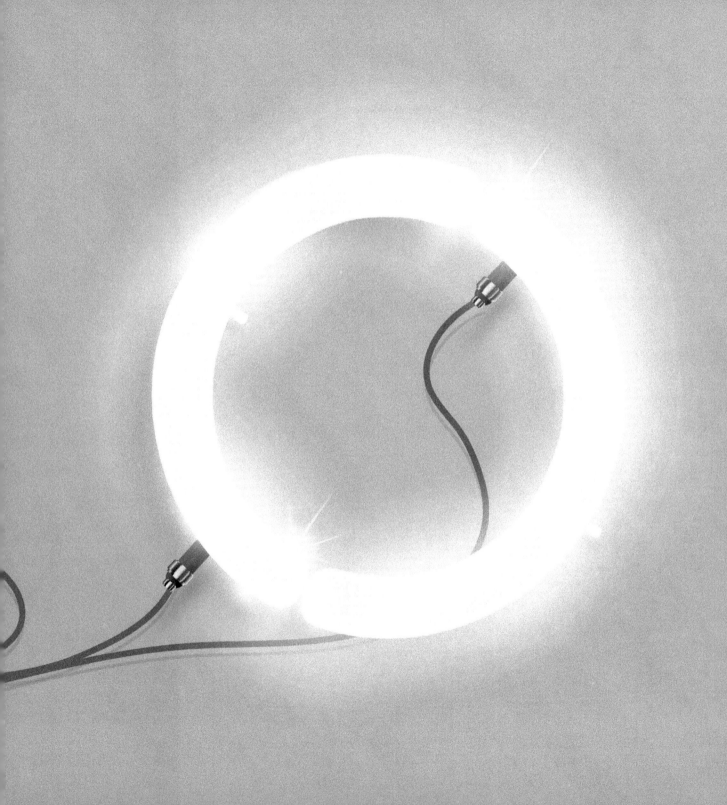

To understand how fluorescent lights work, it's helpful to think about how neon lamps work. Neon lamps are basically glass tubes that have a neon gas inside. When you attach electrical current to the ends of the tube, the electrons inside begin to speed up and then they collide with the atoms of neon. When the collision happens the neon electrons go to energy levels that are higher. When these excited neon electrons return to a lower energy level they create visible light.

Different types of gas create varying colors depending on their energy levels. Neon gas shows up as a red-orange color. If you used vapor from mercury in gas form, it would create a blue-green color. Of course, neither of these colors, which are actually made up of different levels of color, would work for the white light we need. This is where the process of fluorescence comes in.

neon tube

fluorescent lamps

Fluorescence makes it possible for a material to absorb a specific color of light and emit a different color that has a wavelength that's longer. Inside a fluorescent or compact fluorescent light there is a coating that was placed inside the glass. The purpose of that coating is to absorb the light you can't see, the ultraviolet light, and emit it as light you can see—the white light.

There are some disadvantages to these types of lights. If you crack the tube, the gas will escape and the light won't work. In order to get the electrons in the gas excited, the voltage of normal household electricity isn't powerful enough so a ballast that is electromagnetic is used to ramp up the electricity.

fluorescent lamps

incandescent lights

In other words, the lights get hotter than LED lights so they're not as efficient. They used to flicker a lot as well, but today's fluorescent lights don't have that problem so they are good replacements for the older incandescent light bulbs.

INCANDESCENT LIGHTS

When you see a picture of an old-fashioned light bulb, it's an incandescent light. If you look closely at the inside, you'll see that there are two wires. They support a tiny wire on the inside, which is called a filament.

The filament is the piece that Edison and his team worked on throughout many thousands of experiments to get a material that lasted a long time and was practical.

When you turn on the electricity, the wire heats up and then glows. The purpose of the glass bulb around it, is to prevent air from getting in. If the filament encountered air, it would begin to burn and then melt. A melted filament would mean that the bulb wouldn't work any more.

You may wonder why hot things produce light. The truth is that all solid material creates some range of light. An apple on your tabletop produces light. So does the pencil on your desk. The light they produce can't be seen by your eyes. It's infrared light. However, if the object was heated up, then eventually it would produce a wavelength of light that you can see.

The light that the filament gives off is produced by electrons changing energy levels as it was in the previous types of artificial light. The filament is made of a solid material. Its atoms interact with other atoms and the result is that this interaction changes the energy levels of nearby atoms. In fact, there so many different levels of energy that you get all the possible colors, which combine to what our eyes see as white light!

SUMMARY

There are four ways that people can create artificial lighting. Prior to the advent of the electric light bulb, the only way was through creating fire or burning candles. The other three ways to create artificial light all depend on electrical current or battery power. They are incandescent bulbs, like the original Edison light bulb, fluorescent lamps, and LED lights. They all have advantages and disadvantages.

Awesome! Now that you know more about energy, light, and electricity you may want to find out more about how electric motors work in the Baby Professor book How Do Electric Motors Work? Physics Books for Kids.

Visit

BABY PROFESSOR
EDUCATION KIDS

www.BabyProfessorBooks.com
to download Free Baby Professor eBooks
and view our catalog of new and exciting
Children's Books

CPSIA information can be obtained
at www.ICGtesting.com
Printed in the USA
BVHW091433171222
654336BV00011B/474